STEP-BY-STEP
Capitalization and Punctuation

LINWORTH LEARNING

From the Minds of Teachers

Linworth Publishing, Inc.
Worthington, Ohio

Cataloging-in-Publication Data

Editor: Claire Morris

Design and Production: Good Neighbor Press, Inc.

Published by Linworth Publishing, Inc.
480 East Wilson Bridge Road, Suite L
Worthington, Ohio 43085

ISBN: 1-58683-147-X

5 4 3

Table of Contents

Introduction

Step-by-Step Capitalization and Punctuation is designed to motivate and engage students who may have difficulty with language. Skills are addressed in a variety of fun and interesting formats to accommodate individual learning styles. Each skill is introduced according to a developmental progression and at low readability levels to promote success and understanding. Activity sheets have clear and simple instructions, examples,and exercises which may include word manipulation, understanding pictorial cues, and problem-solving. Assessment activities follow the format of standardized tests and require students to eliminate incorrect options, choose the correct answer, and fill in the appropriate circle. The material in this book correlates with the national curriculum standards for Grades 1–2 and covers the following skills: identifying declarative and interrogative sentences, using a period or question mark at the end of sentences, and using knowledge of the basic rules of punctuation and capitalization when reading and writing. An answer key is provided at the back of the book.

Name_____ Date_____

# Introducing Periods

Directions:

Read each sentence.

Decide if the sentence is a telling sentence or not.

Cut out the periods, and glue one to the end of each telling sentence.

1. The sun shines in the sky

2. The sky

3. The stars come out at night

4. The moon is full

5. In the sky

6. The wind blows

Adding Periods

Directions:
Read each sentence.
Write the period in the box.

1. The class walks to the library [.]

2. Jack finds a book about dogs [ ]

3. Grant picks a book on boats [ ]

4. Kate finds a book about rocks [ ]

5. Mindy sees a book about fish [ ]

6. Everyone finds good books [ ]

More Adding Periods

Directions:
Read each sentence.
Write the period in the box.
Draw a picture for the sentence.

1.

The fireman rides in a fire truck ☐

2.

The dog walks in the yard ☐

3.

The man mows the lawn ☐

4.

The woman plants flowers ☐

Ordering Words in Sentences

Directions:
Read each group of words.
Write the words in order to make a sentence
Add a period to the end of the sentence.

1. eat cows grass

   Cows eat grass.

2. climbs the boy the tree

   _____

3. lion the zoo lives the in

   _____

4. swim lake the ducks in

   _____

5. yard in the grow flowers

   _____

6. frog sees he the

   _____

Letter to Grandma

Directions:

Jamal wrote a letter to his grandma.

He forgot to write the periods at the end of each sentence.

Read the letter, and add the periods.

Dear Grandma,

I like to ride bikes ☐

We will visit next week ☐

We can ride when I visit ☐

We can ride to the park ☐

I cannot wait to visit ☐

I will see you soon ☐

Your grandson,

Jamal

Introducing Question Marks

Directions:

Read each sentence.

Decide if the sentence is an asking sentence or not.

Cut out each question mark, and glue it to the end of each asking sentence.

---

1. Can you help me

2 What do

3. How old is Maggie

4. How did you get here

5. Have a party

6. Who came to the game

✂ -

✂
```
┌ ─ ┐        ┌ ─ ┐        ┌ ─ ┐        ┌ ─ ┐
│ ? │        │ ? │        │ ? │        │ ? │
└ ─ ┘        └ ─ ┘        └ ─ ┘        └ ─ ┘
```

Adding Question Marks

Directions:
Read each sentence.
Write the question mark in the box.

1. Where is my bat [?]

2. Have you seen my book [ ]

3. When can I go play [ ]

4. What will you eat for lunch [ ]

5. Do you know Avery [ ]

6. Why does the dog bark [ ]

Ordering Words in Sentences

Directions:

Read each group of words.

Write the words in order to make a sentence.

Add a question mark to the end of the sentence.

---

1. pencil has my who

   <u>Who has my pencil?</u>_____

---

2. going where you are

   _____

---

3. you doing how are

   _____

---

4. seen my have you cat

   _____

---

5. party when is your

   _____

---

6. your is dress this

   _____

More Adding Question Marks

Directions:

Read each sentence.

Add the question mark.

Then answer the question.

1. What is your name

   My name is _____.

2. How old are you

   I am _____ years old.

3. What is your favorite color

   My favorite color is _____.

4. Who is your friend

   My friend is _____.

5. What color are your eyes

   My eyes are _____.

Name_____ Date_____

Books Wanted!

Directions:

Read the ad from the newspaper.
Add the question mark.

Books Wanted

Do you like to read [?]

Do you like books [ ]

What books do you like [ ]

Do you have many books [ ]

Would you like to have more [ ]

Go to your school library and get
a book.

Adding End Marks

Directions:

Read each sentence and decide which end mark it needs.
Cut out the end marks, and glue them to the end of the sentences.

1. Will you be at my party

2 I will go to your party

3. What can I bring

4. You can bring the games

5. It will be fun

6. Can you stay with me

[.]   [?]   [.]   [?]   [.]   [?]

End Marks for Asking and Telling

Directions:

Read each sentence.

Decide which end mark it needs.

Write the end mark.

Write its telling sentence. Write the end mark of the telling sentence.

Word Box

| I can swim well | I will play a game | My Friend is Tim |
| I ride a bike | My hair is brown | |

---

1. Who is your friend

_____

2. What color is your hair

_____

3. Do you ride a bike

_____

4. Will you play a game

_____

5. Can you swim

_____

Name_____ Date_____

Questions and Answers

Directions:
Read each sentence.
Decide which end mark it needs.
Write the end mark.
Then, answer the question.
Add the end mark to the answer.

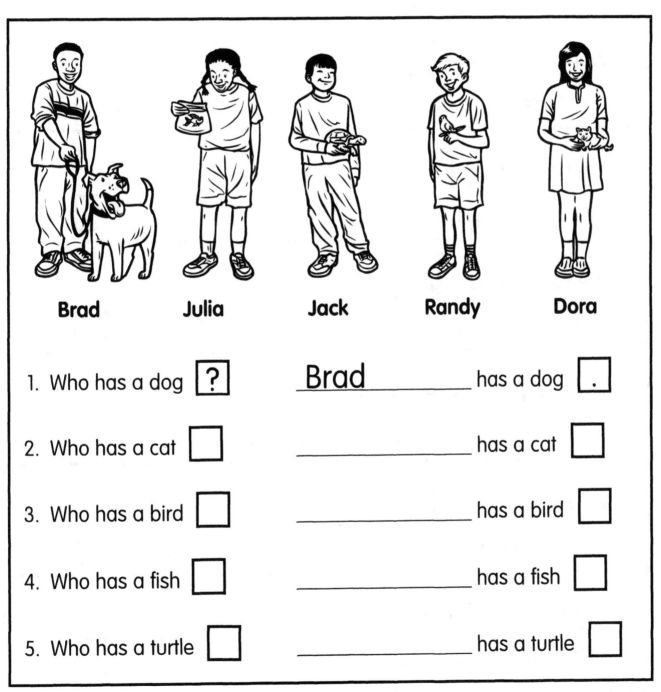

Brad   **Julia**   **Jack**   **Randy**   **Dora**

1. Who has a dog ⟦?⟧   <u>Brad</u> has a dog ⟦.⟧

2. Who has a cat ⟦ ⟧   _____ has a cat ⟦ ⟧

3. Who has a bird ⟦ ⟧   _____ has a bird ⟦ ⟧

4. Who has a fish ⟦ ⟧   _____ has a fish ⟦ ⟧

5. Who has a turtle ⟦ ⟧   _____ has a turtle ⟦ ⟧

Capitalization and Punctuation **13**

More Adding End Marks

Directions:
Read each sentence.
Decide which end mark it needs.
Write the end mark.
Then, answer the question.
Add the end mark to the answer.

1. What is your name $\boxed{?}$

   My name is _____ $\boxed{.}$

2. How old are you $\boxed{}$

   I am _____ $\boxed{}$

3. Are you a boy or a girl $\boxed{}$

   I am a _____ $\boxed{}$

4. What do you like to eat $\boxed{}$

   I like to eat _____ $\boxed{}$

5. Do you like to read $\boxed{}$

   I like to read books about _____ $\boxed{}$

6. What do you like to play $\boxed{}$

   I like to play _____ $\boxed{}$

Reflect and Review

Directions:

Read each group of words.

Cut out each group of words, and glue the words in the correct order.

Write the correct end mark.

1.

2.

3.

4.

✂ -

you	Where	going	are
old	you	are	How
play	We	in	park	the
dad	My	book	a	reads

Introducing Capitalization

Directions:

Read each sentence.

Cut out the letters below.

Glue the letters in the correct boxes so that each sentence begins with a capital letter.

1. ☐ y dog barks.

2. ☐ his is my house.

3. ☐ ho is going with me?

4. ☐ an you help me?

5. ☐ ou are my friend.

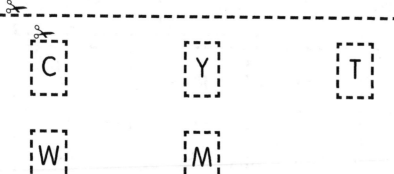

C   Y   T

W   M

Starting Sentences

Directions:

Read each sentence.

Circle each word that is correctly capitalized.

1. (my (My)) mom sings songs.

2. (his, His) dad bakes cakes.

3. (the, The) baby sleeps all day.

4. (Who, who) likes to eat cookies?

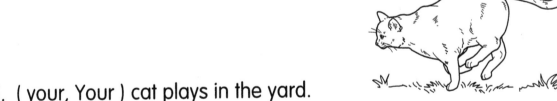

5. (your, Your) cat plays in the yard.

6. (What, what) is her name?

Ordering Words in Sentences

Directions:

Read each group of words.

Cut out each group of words, and glue the words in the correct order.

1.

2.

3.

4.

✂ -

✂

boy	has	The	many	pets.
his	The	man	feeds	cat.
has	birds.	three	The	girl
animals?		Who		likes

Asking Sentences

Directions:

Read each sentence.

Circle the capital letter in the first word of each sentence.

1. (W)ho rides bikes with you?

2. Is the dog barking?

3. Does Maggie like apples?

4. Are Joe's hands clean?

5. What do cows eat?

6. Do you like to play?

More Starting Sentences

Directions:

Read each sentence.

Use the word in front of the blank line to begin the sentence.

Write the word on the line.

1. (this) ___This_____ is fun.

2. (the) _____ dad uses many tools.

3. (a) _____ box holds his tools.

4. (the) _____ hammer hits nails.

5. (an) _____ ax chops wood.

6. (does) _____ your dad like to build things?

Capitalizing *I*

Directions:
Read each sentence.
Circle the word **I** in each sentence.

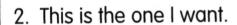

1. Can (I) have a carrot?

2. This is the one I want.

3. Where do I go?

4. Julia and I are friends.

5. I make my lunch for school.

6. What can I bring?

More Capitalizing I

Directions:

Read the sentences.

Cut out each **I** below.

Glue each **I** on an **i** that should be capitalized.

I in Sentences

Directions:
Read each sentence.
Circle the word **I** in each sentence.
Then, draw a line from each sentence to the picture it tells about on the right.

1. Karen and ⓘ eat apples.

2. My mom and I sing songs.

3. My friend and I ride bikes.

4. Jake and I like to read.

5. Maria and I swim in the lake.

More *I* in Sentences

Directions:

Read each sentence.
Circle the correct form of the word.

1. Do ((I), i) know you?

2. Yes, (I, i) know you.

3. What do (I, i) need?

4. This is what (I, i) need.

5. Can (i, I) read this book?

Capitalizing First Names

Directions:

Read each sentence.

Complete each sentence with the correct name.

Make sure the first letter of the name is capitalized.

Maria   **Ellie**   **Todd**   **Kelly**   **Greg**   **Ricky**

1. The girl with the hat is ___Ellie_____ .

2. The boy with the glasses is _____ .

3. The girl with two bows is _____ .

4. The boy with a tie is _____ .

5. The girl who reads a book is _____ .

6. The boy with the cap is _____ .

Family and Friends

Directions:

Read each sentence.

Write the correct first name to complete each sentence.

Draw a picture to go with the sentence.

1. My name is _____ .	2. My mom is _____ .
3. My dad is _____ .	4. My friend is _____ .

More Capitalizing First Nouns

Directions:

Read each sentence.

Circle the capital letter in each first name.

1. (B)rad is my friend.

2. Bill goes to school with Maria.

3. Megan and Jack play on the same team.

4. Joe and Maria play ball with Carlos.

5. Pete has brown hair.

Correct the Sentences

Directions:
Read each sentence.
Circle the capital letter at the beginning of the sentence.
Underline the capital letter in each first name.

1. (T)he dog belongs to <u>J</u>ason.

2. The cake is for Jan's birthday.

3. The dog plays with Andy.

4. How old is Kim?

5. Where does Paul live?

6. Mary rides bikes with Sam.

Identifying Capital Letters

Directions:

Read each sentence.

Circle the capital letter at the beginning of the sentence with a blue crayon.

Circle the capital letter at the beginning of a name with a red crayon.

Circle the word **I** with a yellow crayon.

1. She and I know Jake.

2. I gave the book to Ming.

3. Where can I find Juan?

4. Julie knows I like Jack.

5. My mom and I met Pam.

Reflect and Review

Directions:

Read each sentence.

Circle the capital letter at the beginning of the sentence with a blue crayon.

Circle the capital letter at the beginning of a name with a red crayon.

Circle the word **I** with a yellow crayon.

1. My friend and I know Rob.

2. Jenny and I play ball with Sandra.

3. Am I on a team with Scott?

4. Can I sit by Greg?

5. Kari and I eat lunch with Luke.

6. Will Meg and I go the the game?

Assessment 1

Directions:

Read each sentence.

Fill in the circle for the sentence that is punctuated correctly.

1. ● The girl walks the dog.

   ○ The boy rides his bike

2. ○ My cat sleeps on my bed.

   ○ My cat sleeps on my bed

3. ○ His dad reads a book.

   ○ His dad reads a book

4. ○ I see stars at night

   ○ I see stars at night.

5. ○ My friend jumps rope.

   ○ My friend jumps rope?

6. ○ We jump rope

   ○ We jump rope.

Assessment 2

Directions:

Read each sentence.

Fill in the circle for the sentence that is punctuated correctly.

1. ● Who is he?

   ○ Who is he.

2. ○ Where are you going.

   ○ Where are you going?

3. ○ How old are you?

   ○ How old are you.

4. ○ Who helped you?

   ○ Who helped you.

5. ○ What do you see.

   ○ What do you see?

6. ○ Why do you ask.

   ○ Why do you ask?

Assessment 3

Directions:

Read each sentence.

Fill in the circle for the sentence that is punctuated correctly.

1. ● The dog runs.

   ○ Does she eat apples.

   ○ How do you know.

2. ○ Do you have a dog?

   ○ I have a dog?

   ○ I read books about dogs?

3. ○ Can you run?

   ○ I can skip?

   ○ I can run?

4. ○ Did she call you.

   ○ My friend talks to me.

   ○ Does she talk a lot.

5. ○ I read books?

   ○ Do you read books?

   ○ I read short books?

Assessment 4

Directions:

Read each sentence.

Fill in the circle for the sentence that is not punctuated correctly.

1. ● He tells me?

   ○ Do you have it?

   ○ Are we going know?

2. ○ Where are you going?

   ○ Who asked for help?

   ○ I am going to school?

3. ○ My friend plays ball.

   ○ Do you play ball.

   ○ I like baseball.

4. ○ Who is going to the park.

   ○ I will swing.

   ○ He will go down the slide.

5. ○ Can you ride a bike?

   ○ Will you ride bikes with me?

   ○ I can ride bikes with you?

Assessment 5

Directions:

Read each sentence.

Fill in the circle under the correct form of the word.

---

1. Who will (I, i) invite?

         I   i

         ●   ○

---

2. This is the one (I, i) like.

         I   i

         ○   ○

---

3. Where am (I, i) going?

         I   i

         ○   ○

---

4. My mom and (I, i) play games.

         I   i

         ○   ○

---

5. Who do (I, i) need to help?

         I   i

         ○   ○

---

6. Can (I, i) call you?

         I   i

         ○   ○

Assessment 6

Directions:

Read each sentence.

Fill in the circle under the word that is capitalized correctly.

---

1. The Girl is my best Friend.

   The   Girl   Friend
   ●   ○   ○

---

2. The frog Jumps in the Pond.

   The   Jumps   Pond
   ○   ○   ○

---

3. My Dog likes to Chase cats.

   My   Dog   Chase
   ○   ○   ○

---

4. Who knows Where my Book is?

   Who   Where   Book
   ○   ○   ○

---

5. I like playing with This Toy.

   I   This   Toy
   ○   ○   ○

---

6. When can She come Over here?

   When   She   Over
   ○   ○   ○

Assessment 7

Directions:
Read each sentence.
Fill in the circle under the word that is not capitalized correctly.

---

1. Rick and I are Friends.

   Rick   I   Friends
   ○   ○   ●

---

2. My friend and I Watch a movie.

   My   I   Watch
   ○   ○   ○

---

3. The boy Plays ball with Kelly.

   The   Plays   Kelly
   ○   ○   ○

---

4. My sister and I Hide by a tree.

   My   I   Hide
   ○   ○   ○

---

5. The Dog barks at Sarah.

   The   Dog   Sarah
   ○   ○   ○

---

6. The teacher Reads to Jamal.

   The   Reads   Jamal
   ○   ○   ○

Assessment 8

Directions:

Read each sentence.

Fill in the circle next to the correct word.

1. (Who, who) are you?	● Who ○ who
2. (the, The) boy plays ball.	○ the ○ The
3. (this, This) class is fun.	○ this ○ This
4. (the, The) fish swims in a tank.	○ the ○ The
5. (My, my) mom drives me to school.	○ My ○ my
6. (an, An) ant bit my foot.	○ an ○ An

Assessment 9

Directions:
Read each sentence.
Fill in the circle for the sentence that is capitalized correctly.

---

1. ● The cat sleeps.

   ○ the cat Sleeps.

   ○ the Cat sleeps.

---

2. ○ The Dog barks.

   ○ The dog barks.

   ○ the Dog barks.

---

3. ○ My name is chris.

   ○ My Name is Chris.

   ○ My name is Chris.

---

4. ○ Jake says I draw well.

   ○ Jake says i draw well.

   ○ jake says I draw well.

---

5. ○ lisa and I are friends.

   ○ Lisa and I are friends.

   ○ Lisa and i are friends.

Introducing Periods

Directions:
Read each sentence.
Decide if the sentence is a telling sentence or not.
Cut out the periods, and glue one to the end of each telling sentence.

1. The sun shines in the sky [.]
2. The sky
3. The stars come out at night [.]
4. The moon is full [.]
5. In the sky
6. The wind blows [.]

[.] [.] [.] [.]

Adding Periods

Directions:
Read each sentence.
Write the period in the box.

1. The class walks to the library [.]
2. Jack finds a book about dogs [.]
3. Grant picks a book on boats [.]
4. Kate finds a book about rocks [.]
5. Mindy sees a book about fish [.]
6. Everyone finds good books [.]

More Adding Periods

Directions:
Read each sentence.
Write the period in the box.
Draw a picture for the sentence.

1. The fireman rides in a fire truck [.]
2. The dog walks in the yard [.]
3. The man mows the lawn [.]
4. The woman plants flowers [.]

Ordering Words in Sentences

Directions:
Read each group of words.
Write the words in order to make a sentence
Add a period to the end of the sentence.

1. eat cows grass
   Cows eat grass.
2. climbs the boy the tree
   The boy climbs the tree.
3. lion the zoo lives the in
   The lion lives in the zoo.
4. swim lake the ducks in
   The ducks swim in the lake.
5. yard in the grow flowers
   The flowers grow in the yard.
6. frog sees he the
   He sees the frog.

Letter to Grandma

Directions:
Jamal wrote a letter to his grandma.
He forgot to write the periods at the end of each sentence.
Read the letter, and add the periods.

Dear Grandma,

I like to ride bikes [.]

We will visit next week [.]

We can ride when I visit [.]

We can ride to the park [.]

I cannot wait to visit [.]

I will see you soon [.]

Your grandson,

Jamal

Introducing Question Marks

Directions:
Read each sentence.
Decide if the sentence is an asking sentence or not.
Cut out each question mark, and glue it to the end of each asking sentence.

1. Can you help me [?]
2. What do
3. How old is Maggie [?]
4. How did you get here [?]
5. Have a party
6. Who came to the game [?]

[?] [?] [?] [?]

Adding Question Marks

Directions:
Read each sentence.
Write the question mark in the box.

1. Where is my bat [?]
2. Have you seen my book [?]
3. When can I go play [?]
4. What will you eat for lunch [?]
5. Do you know Avery [?]
6. Why does the dog bark [?]

Ordering Words in Sentences

Directions:
Read each group of words.
Write the words in order to make a sentence.
Add a question mark to the end of the sentence.

1. pencil has my who
   Who has my pencil?
2. going where you are
   Where are you going?
3. you doing how are
   How are you doing?
4. seen my have you cat
   Have you seen my cat?
5. party when is your
   When is your party?
6. your is dress this
   Is this your dress?

More Adding Question Marks

Directions:
Read each sentence.
Add the question mark.
Then answer the question.

1. What is your name?
   My name is ___
2. How old are you?
   I am ___ years old.
3. What is your favorite color?
   My favorite color is ___
4. Who is your friend?
   My friend is ___
5. What color are your eyes?
   My eyes are ___

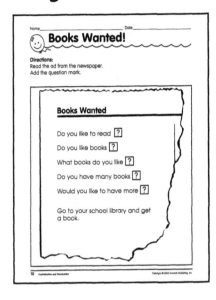

Books Wanted!

Directions:
Read the ad from the newspaper.
Add the question mark.

Books Wanted

Do you like to read [?]

Do you like books [?]

What books do you like [?]

Do you have many books [?]

Would you like to have more [?]

Go to your school library and get a book.

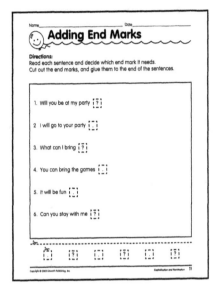

Adding End Marks

Directions:
Read each sentence and decide which end mark it needs.
Cut out the end marks, and glue them to the end of the sentences.

1. Will you be at my party [?]

2. I will go to your party [.]

3. What can I bring [?]

4. You can bring the games [.]

5. It will be fun [.]

6. Can you stay with me [?]

[.] [?] [.] [?] [.] [?]

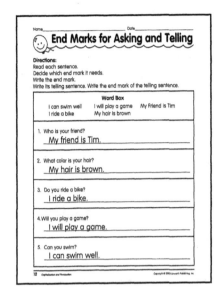

End Marks for Asking and Telling

Directions:
Read each sentence.
Decide which end mark it needs.
Write the end mark.
Write its telling sentence. Write the end mark of the telling sentence.

Word Box

I can swim well	I will play a game	My Friend is Tim
I ride a bike	My hair is brown	

1. Who is your friend?
   My friend is Tim.

2. What color is your hair?
   My hair is brown.

3. Do you ride a bike?
   I ride a bike.

4. Will you play a game?
   I will play a game.

5. Can you swim?
   I can swim well.

Questions and Answers

Directions:
Read each sentence.
Decide which end mark it needs.
Write the end mark.
Then, answer the question.
Add the end mark to the answer.

Brad   Julia   Jack   Randy   Dora

1. Who has a dog [?]   Brad   has a dog [.]

2. Who has a cat [?]   Dora   has a cat [.]

3. Who has a bird [?]   Randy   has a bird [.]

4. Who has a fish [?]   Julia   has a fish [.]

5. Who has a turtle [?]   Jack   has a turtle [.]

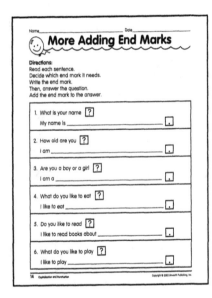

More Adding End Marks

Directions:
Read each sentence.
Decide which end mark it needs.
Write the end mark.
Then, answer the question.
Add the end mark to the answer.

1. What is your name [?]
   My name is _____ [.]

2. How old are you [?]
   I am _____ [.]

3. Are you a boy or a girl [?]
   I am a _____ [.]

4. What do you like to eat [?]
   I like to eat _____ [.]

5. Do you like to read [?]
   I like to read books about _____ [.]

6. What do you like to play [?]
   I like to play _____ [.]

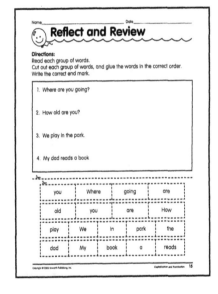

Reflect and Review

Directions:
Read each group of words.
Cut out each group of words, and glue the words in the correct order.
Write the correct end mark.

1. Where are you going?

2. How old are you?

3. We play in the park.

4. My dad reads a book.

you	Where	going	are
old	you	are	How
play	We	in	park	the
dad	My	book	a	reads

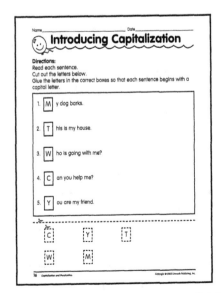

Introducing Capitalization

Directions:
Read each sentence.
Cut out the letters below.
Glue the letters in the correct boxes so that each sentence begins with a capital letter.

1. [M] y dog barks.

2. [T] his is my house.

3. [W] ho is going with me?

4. [C] an you help me?

5. [Y] ou are my friend.

[C] [Y] [T]

[W] [M]

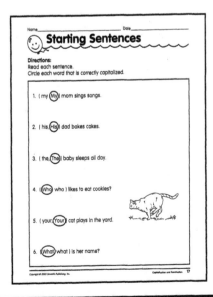

Starting Sentences

Directions:
Read each sentence.
Circle each word that is correctly capitalized.

1. (my (My)) mom sings songs.

2. (his, (His)) dad bakes cakes.

3. (the, (The)) baby sleeps all day.

4. ((Who) who) likes to eat cookies?

5. (your, (Your)) cat plays in the yard.

6. ((What) what) is her name?

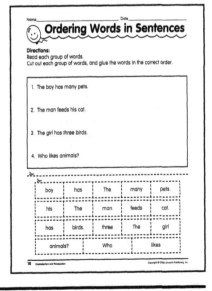

Ordering Words in Sentences

Directions:
Read each group of words.
Cut out each group of words, and glue the words in the correct order.

1. The boy has many pets.

2. The man feeds his cat.

3. The girl has three birds.

4. Who likes animals?

boy	has	The	many	pets.
his	The	man	feeds	cat.
has	birds.	three	The	girl
animals?	Who		likes	

Answer Key pages 19-27

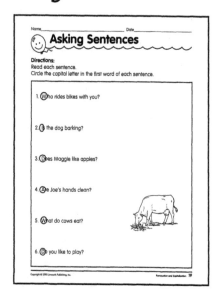

Asking Sentences

Directions:
Read each sentence.
Circle the capital letter in the first word of each sentence.

1. (W)ho rides bikes with you?

2. (I)s the dog barking?

3. (D)oes Maggie like apples?

4. (A)re Joe's hands clean?

5. (W)hat do cows eat?

6. (D)o you like to play?

Copyright © 2003 Linworth Publishing, Inc.   Punctuation and Capitalization 19

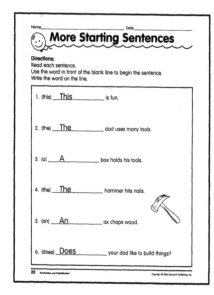

More Starting Sentences

Directions:
Read each sentence.
Use the word in front of the blank line to begin the sentence.
Write the word on the line.

1. (this) __This__ is fun.

2. (the) __The__ dad uses many tools.

3. (a) __A__ box holds his tools.

4. (the) __The__ hammer hits nails.

5. (an) __An__ ax chops wood.

6. (does) __Does__ your dad like to build things?

20 Punctuation and Capitalization   Copyright © 2003 Linworth Publishing, Inc.

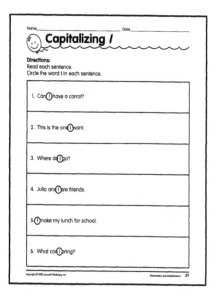

Capitalizing I

Directions:
Read each sentence.
Circle the word I in each sentence.

1. Can (I) have a carrot?

2. This is the one (I) want.

3. Where do (I) go?

4. Julia and (I) are friends.

5. (I) make my lunch for school.

6. What can (I) bring?

Copyright © 2003 Linworth Publishing, Inc.   Punctuation and Capitalization 21

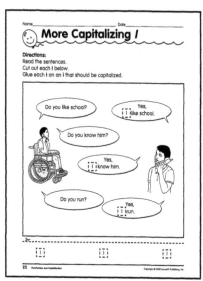

More Capitalizing I

Directions:
Read the sentences.
Cut out each I below.
Glue each I on an i that should be capitalized.

Do you like school?   Yes, I like school.

Do you know him?

Yes, I know him.

Do you run?   Yes, I run.

22 Punctuation and Capitalization   Copyright © 2003 Linworth Publishing, Inc.

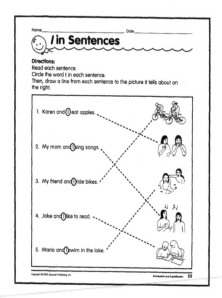

I in Sentences

Directions:
Read each sentence.
Circle the word I in each sentence.
Then, draw a line from each sentence to the picture it tells about on the right.

1. Karen and (I) eat apples.

2. My mom and (I) sing songs.

3. My friend and (I) ride bikes.

4. Jake and (I) like to read.

5. Maria and (I) swim in the lake.

Copyright © 2003 Linworth Publishing, Inc.   Punctuation and Capitalization 23

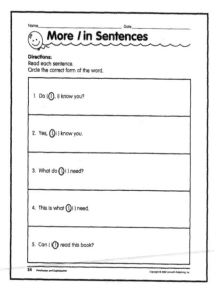

More I in Sentences

Directions:
Read each sentence.
Circle the correct form of the word.

1. Do (I, i) know you?

2. Yes, (I, i) know you.

3. What do (I, i) need?

4. This is what (I, i) need.

5. Can (I, i) read this book?

24 Punctuation and Capitalization   Copyright © 2003 Linworth Publishing, Inc.

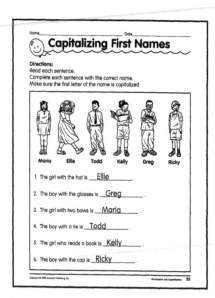

Capitalizing First Names

Directions:
Read each sentence.
Complete each sentence with the correct name.
Make sure the first letter of the name is capitalized.

Maria   Ellie   Todd   Kelly   Greg   Ricky

1. The girl with the hat is __Ellie__

2. The boy with the glasses is __Greg__

3. The girl with two bows is __Maria__

4. The boy with a tie is __Todd__

5. The girl who reads a book is __Kelly__

6. The boy with the cap is __Ricky__

Copyright © 2003 Linworth Publishing, Inc.   Punctuation and Capitalization 25

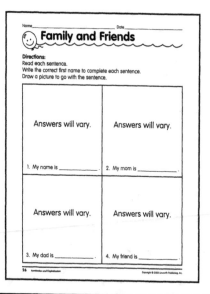

Family and Friends

Directions:
Read each sentence.
Write the correct first name to complete each sentence.
Draw a picture to go with the sentence.

Answers will vary.	Answers will vary.
1. My name is _____	2. My mom is _____
Answers will vary.	Answers will vary.
3. My dad is _____	4. My friend is _____

26 Punctuation and Capitalization   Copyright © 2003 Linworth Publishing, Inc.

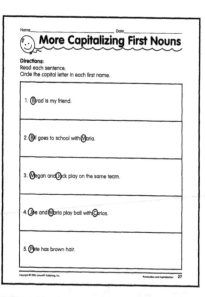

More Capitalizing First Nouns

Directions:
Read each sentence.
Circle the capital letter in each first name.

1. (B)rad is my friend.

2. (B)ill goes to school with (M)aria.

3. (M)egan and (J)ack play on the same team.

4. (J)oe and (M)aria play ball with (C)arlos.

5. (P)ete has brown hair.

Copyright © 2003 Linworth Publishing, Inc.   Punctuation and Capitalization 27

Answer Key pages 28-36

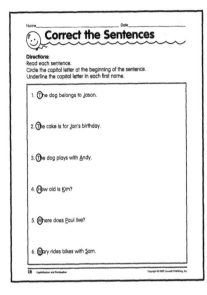

Correct the Sentences

Directions:
Read each sentence.
Circle the capital letter at the beginning of the sentence.
Underline the capital letter in each first name.

1. (T)he dog belongs to _Jason_.

2. (T)he cake is for _Jan's_ birthday.

3. (T)he dog plays with _Andy_.

4. (H)ow old is _Kim_?

5. (W)here does _Paul_ live?

6. (M)ary rides bikes with _Sam_.

28 Capitalization and Punctuation

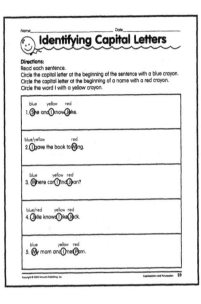

Identifying Capital Letters

Directions:
Read each sentence.
Circle the capital letter at the beginning of the sentence with a blue crayon.
Circle the capital letter at the beginning of a name with a red crayon.
Circle the word I with a yellow crayon.

blue   yellow   red
1. (S)he and (I) know (J)ake.

blue/yellow   red
2. (I) gave the book to (M)ing.

blue   yellow   red
3. (W)here can (I) find (J)van?

blue/red   yellow   red
4. (J)llie knows (I) like (J)ack.

blue   yellow   red
5. (M)y mom and (I) met (P)am.

29 Capitalization and Punctuation

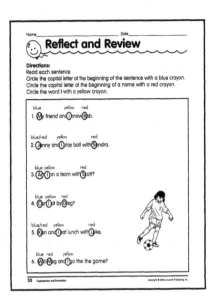

Reflect and Review

Directions:
Read each sentence.
Circle the capital letter at the beginning of the sentence with a blue crayon.
Circle the capital letter at the beginning of a name with a red crayon.
Circle the word I with a yellow crayon.

blue   yellow   red
1. (M)y friend and (I) know (R)ob.

blue/red   yellow   red
2. (J)enny and (I) play ball with (S)andra.

blue   yellow   red
3. (A)m (I) on a team with (S)cott?

blue   yellow   red
4. (C)an (I) sit by (G)reg?

blue/red   yellow   red
5. (K)ari and (I) eat lunch with (L)uke.

blue   red   yellow
6. (W)ill (M)eg and (I) go the the game?

30 Capitalization and Punctuation

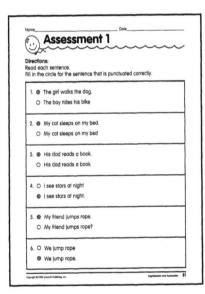

Assessment 1

Directions:
Read each sentence.
Fill in the circle for the sentence that is punctuated correctly.

1. ● The girl walks the dog.
   ○ The boy rides his bike

2. ● My cat sleeps on my bed.
   ○ My cat sleeps on my bed

3. ● His dad reads a book.
   ○ His dad reads a book

4. ○ I see stars at night
   ● I see stars at night.

5. ● My friend jumps rope.
   ○ My friend jumps rope

6. ○ We jump rope
   ● We jump rope.

31 Capitalization and Punctuation

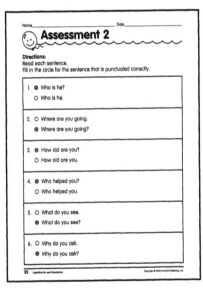

Assessment 2

Directions:
Read each sentence.
Fill in the circle for the sentence that is punctuated correctly.

1. ● Who is he?
   ○ Who is he.

2. ○ Where are you going.
   ● Where are you going?

3. ● How old are you?
   ○ How old are you.

4. ● Who helped you?
   ○ Who helped you.

5. ○ What do you see.
   ● What do you see?

6. ○ Why do you ask.
   ● Why do you ask?

32 Capitalization and Punctuation

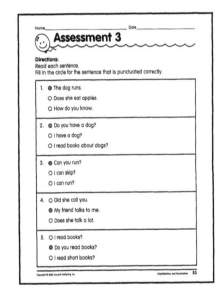

Assessment 3

Directions:
Read each sentence.
Fill in the circle for the sentence that is punctuated correctly.

1. ● The dog runs.
   ○ Does she eat apples.
   ○ How do you know.

2. ● Do you have a dog?
   ○ i have a dog?
   ○ I read books about dogs?

3. ● Can you run?
   ○ i can skip?
   ○ i can run?

4. ○ Did she call you.
   ● My friend talks to me.
   ○ Does she talk a lot.

5. ○ I read books?
   ● Do you read books?
   ○ I read short books?

33 Capitalization and Punctuation

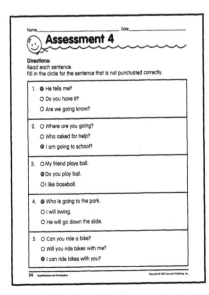

Assessment 4

Directions:
Read each sentence.
Fill in the circle for the sentence that is not punctuated correctly.

1. ● He tells me?
   ○ Do you have it?
   ○ Are we going know?

2. ● Where are you going?
   ○ Who asked for help?
   ● I am going to school?

3. ○ My friend plays ball.
   ● Do you play ball.
   ○ I like baseball.

4. ● Who is going to the park.
   ○ I will swing.
   ○ He will go down the slide.

5. ● Can you ride a bike?
   ○ Will you ride bikes with me?
   ● I can ride bikes with you?

34 Capitalization and Punctuation

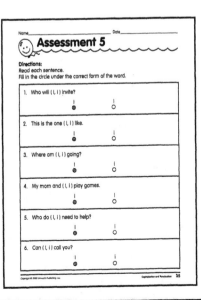

Assessment 5

Directions:
Read each sentence.
Fill in the circle under the correct form of the word.

1. Who will (I, i) invite?
   ●   ○

2. This is the one (I, i) like.
   ●   ○

3. Where am (I, i) going?
   ●   ○

4. My mom and (I, i) play games.
   ●   ○

5. Who do (I, i) need to help?
   ●   ○

6. Can (I, i) call you?
   ●   ○

35 Capitalization and Punctuation

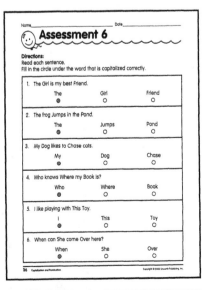

Assessment 6

Directions:
Read each sentence.
Fill in the circle under the word that is capitalized correctly.

1. The Girl is my best Friend.		
The ●	Girl ○	Friend ○
2. The frog Jumps in the Pond.		
The ●	Jumps ○	Pond ○
3. My Dog likes to Chase cats.		
My ●	Dog ○	Chase ○
4. Who knows Where my Book is?		
Who ●	Where ○	Book ○
5. I like playing with This Toy.		
I ●	This ○	Toy ○
6. When can She come Over here?		
When ●	She ○	Over ○

36 Capitalization and Punctuation

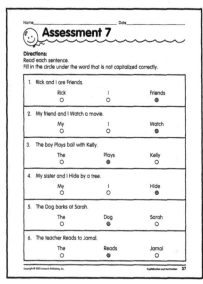

Name_____ Date_____

Assessment 7

Directions:
Read each sentence.
Fill in the circle under the word that is not capitalized correctly.

1. Rick and I are Friends.

Rick	I	Friends
○	○	●

2. My friend and I Watch a movie.

My	I	Watch
○	○	●

3. The boy Plays ball with Kelly.

The	Plays	Kelly
○	●	○

4. My sister and I Hide by a tree.

My	I	Hide
○	○	●

5. The Dog barks at Sarah.

The	Dog	Sarah
○	●	○

6. The teacher Reads to Jamal.

The	Reads	Jamal
○	●	○

Copyright © 2003 Linworth Publishing, Inc.   Capitalization and Punctuation   **37**

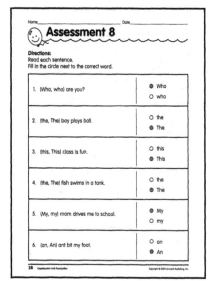

Name_____ Date_____

Assessment 8

Directions:
Read each sentence.
Fill in the circle next to the correct word.

1. (Who, who) are you?

   ● Who
   ○ who

2. (the, The) boy plays ball.

   ○ the
   ● The

3. (this, This) class is fun.

   ○ this
   ● This

4. (the, The) fish swims in a tank.

   ○ the
   ● The

5. (My, my) mom drives me to school.

   ● My
   ○ my

6. (an, An) ant bit my foot.

   ○ an
   ● An

38   Capitalization and Punctuation   Copyright © 2003 Linworth Publishing, Inc.

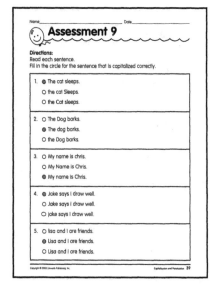

Name_____ Date_____

Assessment 9

Directions:
Read each sentence.
Fill in the circle for the sentence that is capitalized correctly.

1. ● The cat sleeps.
   ○ the cat Sleeps.
   ○ the Cat sleeps.

2. ○ The Dog barks.
   ● The dog barks.
   ○ the Dog barks.

3. ○ My name is chris.
   ○ My Name is Chris.
   ● My name is Chris.

4. ● Jake says I draw well.
   ○ Jake says i draw well.
   ○ jake says I draw well.

5. ○ lisa and I are friends.
   ● Lisa and I are friends.
   ○ Lisa and I are friends.

Copyright © 2003 Linworth Publishing, Inc.   Capitalization and Punctuation   **39**

Printed in the USA
CPSIA information can be obtained
at www.ICGtesting.com
LVHW080724170724
785510LV00007B/293

9 781586 831479